Frida Kahlo in Fort Lauderdale

Frida Kahlo
in Fort Lauderdale

POEMS

BY

Stephen Gibson

ABLE MUSE PRESS

Copyright ©2024 by Stephen Gibson
First published in 2024 by

Able Muse Press

www.ablemusepress.com

All rights reserved. No part of this book may be used or reproduced in any manner whatsoever without written permission except in the case of brief quotations embedded in critical articles and reviews. Requests for permission should be addressed to the Able Muse Press editor at editor@ablemuse.com

Printed in the United States of America

Library of Congress Cataloging-in-Publication Data

Names: Gibson, Stephen, 1948- author.
Title: Frida Kahlo in Fort Lauderdale : poems / by Stephen Gibson.
Description: San Jose, CA : Able Muse Press, 2024.
Identifiers: LCCN 2020056508 (print) | LCCN 2020056509
   (ebook) | ISBN 9781773491615 (hardback) | ISBN
   9781773490922 (paperback) | ISBN 9781773490915 (ebook)
Subjects: LCGFT: Poetry.
Classification: LCC PS3557.I225 F75 2021 (print) | LCC PS3557.
   I225 (ebook) | DDC 811/.54--dc23
LC record available at https://lccn.loc.gov/2020056508
LC ebook record available at https://lccn.loc.gov/2020056509

Cover image: *Kahlo Framed* by Alexander Pepple
   (with *Gray Panel* by Cottonbro, *Frond* by ClipartMax, and *Self-Portrait on the Borderline between Mexico and the United States* by Frida Kahlo)

Cover & book design by Alexander Pepple

Stephen Gibson photo (on page 60) by Cloe V. Gibson

Able Muse Press is an imprint of
   Able Muse: A Review of Poetry, Prose & Art—
   at www.ablemuse.com

Able Muse Press
467 Saratoga Avenue #602
San Jose, CA 95129

*For my wife, Cloe,
my son, Joseph,
my daughter, Kyla, and
her husband, Chris*

Acknowledgments

Grateful acknowledgment is made to the editors of the following publications in which these poems, or earlier versions, first appeared:

The Laurel Review: "Frida Kahlo's Painting *Remembrance of the Open Wound*"

Measure: "Frida Kahlo's Painting *Henry Ford Hospital* (Also Called *The Flying Bed*)"—instance with first line "It isn't that the body needs it to live."

Raleigh Review: "Frida Kahlo's Lead Pencil Drawing of Her Bus Collision with the Trolley" and "Frida Kahlo's Teen Boyfriend's Memory of Her Bus-Trolley Collision"

Salamander: "Frida Kahlo's Painting *The Deceased Dimas Rosas Aged Three*"

Thanks to Brad Leithauser, 2020 Able Muse Book Award final judge, for selecting this collection as a finalist. Thanks also to those at Able Muse Press for their dedication and expertise. Finally, my deepest gratitude to Alexander Pepple for making this book a reality—thank you, Alex.

Contents

Frida Kahlo in Fort Lauderdale

- *vii* Acknowledgments
- *3* Gift Shop Frida Kahlo
- *4* Close-up Photo of Diego Rivera's Eyeball, Attributed to Frida Kahlo
- *5* Photo of Diego Rivera Posing beside a Giant Papier-Mâché Devil
- *6* Frida Kahlo's Colored Pencil Drawing of Her Bus Collision with a Trolley
- *7* Frida Kahlo's Painting *The Deceased Dimas Rosas Aged Three*
- *8* Frida Kahlo's Photo of Diego Rivera with Pet Parrot
- *9* Frida Kahlo's Painting *Self-Portrait II*
- *10* Frida Kahlo's Photo of Diego Rivera with Pet Spider Monkey
- *11* Frida Kahlo's Lead Pencil Drawing of Her Bus Collision with the Trolley
- *12* Frida Kahlo's Photo of Diego Rivera at La Casa Azul
- *13* Héctor García's Photo of Frida Kahlo Asleep with Her Hairless Xoloitzcuintli Dog
- *14* Frida Kahlo's Painting *Remembrance of the Open Wound*
- *15* Frida Kahlo's Painting *Self-Portrait in a Velvet Dress*
- *16* Frida Kahlo's Painting *Henry Ford Hospital* (Also Called *The Flying Bed*)

17 Frida Kahlo's Painting *Henry Ford Hospital* (Also Called *The Flying Bed*)
18 Frida Kahlo's Painting *Without Hope*
19 Photo of Frida Kahlo with Butchered Hair and Wearing Male Attire
20 Frida Kahlo's *Self-Portrait Very Ugly*
21 Frida Kahlo's Self-Portrait *Itzcuintli Dog with Me*
22 Frida Kahlo's Self-Portrait *Fulang-Chang and I*
23 Tabloid Photo of Diego Rivera with Hollywood Actress Paulette Goddard
24 Frida Kahlo's Painting *Self-Portrait with Cropped Hair*
25 Frida Kahlo's Self-Portrait *Diego and I*
26 André Breton's Picnic Photo of Leon Trotsky, Trotsky's Wife Natalia Sedova, Diego Rivera, Frida Kahlo, and Himself
27 Frida Kahlo's Painting *Between the Curtains* (Dedicated to Trotsky)
28 Nickolas Muray's Photo of Frida Kahlo with Her Pet Deer
29 Nickolas Muray's Photo of Frida Kahlo with Chavela Vargas
30 Colored Pencil Drawing of Frida Kahlo's Bus-Trolley Collision
31 Frida Kahlo's Teen Boyfriend's Memory of Her Bus-Trolley Collision
32 Frida Kahlo's Painting *The Suicide of Dorothy Hale*
33 Frida Kahlo's Painting *The Suicide of Dorothy Hale*
34 Frida Kahlo's Nude Self-Portrait with Back Brace *The Broken Column*
35 Photo of Frida Kahlo in Wheelchair Painting Her Self-Portrait *The Broken Column*
36 Frida Kahlo's Self-Portraits with Her Parrots
37 Frida Kahlo's Painting *Self-Portrait with Doll*
38 Frida Kahlo's Painting *A Few Small Nips* (*Passionately in Love*)

39 Frida Kahlo's Painting *Portrait of Diego Rivera*
40 Photo of Frida Kahlo Flanked by Leon Trotsky and His Wife Natalia Sedova
41 Deathbed Hospital Photo of Leon Trotsky
42 Photo of Frida Kahlo in Body Cast Painted with Soviet Hammer and Sickle
43 Frida Kahlo Photographed by Caricaturist Miguel Covarrubias
44 Photo of Diego Rivera and Frida Kahlo Reunited at La Casa Azul
45 Photo of Frida Kahlo, Diego Rivera, and Pet Spider Monkey
46 Photo of Frida Kahlo and Dr. Farill beside Her Painting *Self-Portrait with the Portrait of Dr. Farill*
47 Wallace Marly's Photo of Frida Kahlo and Diego Rivera Reunited
48 Late Photo of Frida Kahlo Propped Up in Bed Painting as Diego Rivera Looks On
49 Late Frida Kahlo's Colored Pencil Drawing of the Bus-Trolley Accident
50 Frida Kahlo's Self-Portraits with Her Parrots
51 Late Photo of Frida Kahlo in Her Wheelchair
52 Julien Levy's Photo of Frida Kahlo Looking Off into the Distance
53 Photo of Diego Rivera at Frida Kahlo's Deathbed
54 Photo of Young Frida Kahlo beside Diego Rivera Seated in Chair with Stetson on His Knee
55 Frida Kahlo's Painting *Girl with Death Mask (She Plays Alone)*
56 Self-Portrait Photo of Frida Kahlo at Her Reflection Pool
57 Frida Kahlo's Painting *Tree of Hope*
58 Gisèle Freund's Photo of Frida Kahlo at La Casa Azul
59 Photo of Frida Kahlo's Casket Being Carried from the Palace of Fine Arts

Frida Kahlo in Fort Lauderdale

*There have been two great accidents in my life.
One was the trolley, and the other was Diego.
Diego was by far the worst.*

—Frida Kahlo

Gift Shop Frida Kahlo

Frida Kahlo, *Self-Portrait with Monkeys*, 1943

She stares at us with her affectionate monkeys
grasping her arms and neck on a food trivet.
Sans eyebrow/upper lip wax or mani/pedi,
she stares at us with her affectionate monkeys.
It's Fort Lauderdale's Rivera/Kahlo exhibit:
Diego? Inflated. Frida? Outrageous, messy.
She stares at us with her affectionate monkeys
grasping her arms and neck on a food trivet.

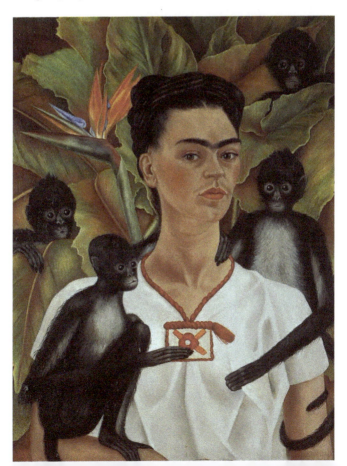

Close-up Photo of Diego Rivera's Eyeball, Attributed to Frida Kahlo

Frida Kahlo, *Diego Rivera's Eye*, 1936

Diego shot out a phonograph at a party.
Frida wondered what she needed to impress
(she learned she had only to take off her dress).
Diego shot out a phonograph at a party.
But nothing has meaning if no one can see
so a camera records her miserable happiness.
Diego shot out a phonograph at a party.
Frida wondered what she needed to impress.

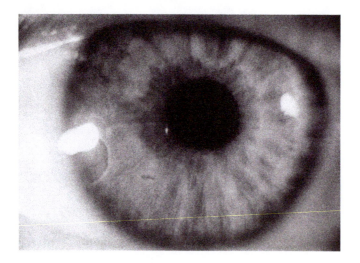

Photo of Diego Rivera Posing beside a Giant Papier-Mâché Devil

Lucienne Bloch, *Diego Rivera Posing with Giant Papier-Mâché Devil and Girl*, 1931

Diego said there was more feeling in his handshake
than with most women when they were having sex.
Frida knew when she married him what to expect:
Diego said there was more feeling in his handshake.
Women confused love with fidelity—their mistake:
monogamy was a leash and collar around his neck.
Diego said there was more feeling in his handshake
than with most women when they were having sex.

For the photograph, search online with the title string, or go to https://www.green-coursehub.com/research-blog/emblematic-giants-and-virtuous-curiosities-diego-riveras-personal-collections (scroll down).

Frida Kahlo's Colored Pencil Drawing of Her Bus Collision with a Trolley

Frida Kahlo, *The Bus Accident*, 1926

Red—unzip her torso and take a look inside.
Black—the grackles always waiting to feed.
Blue—the Madonna hovering in the blue sky.
Red—unzip her torso and take a look inside.
Green—the false hope arising out of need.
Orange—the color of corpses; don't even try.
Red—unzip her torso and take a look inside.
Black—the grackles always waiting to feed.

Frida Kahlo's Painting *The Deceased Dimas Rosas Aged Three*

1937

Diego painted the mother cradling him.
Frida painted him as he was in death—
eyelids parted (hold a mirror: no breath).
Diego painted the mother cradling him.
The mother believed in prayer, and sin.
Frida believed in doctors, not witchcraft.
Diego painted the mother cradling him.
Frida painted him as he was in death.

Frida Kahlo's Photo of Diego Rivera with Pet Parrot

Diego feels like the parrot, trained to say back
whatever she needs to hear, though meaningless—
he was her tutor in everything, like how to dress:
now, he's become the parrot trained to talk back.
Of women—including her sister—there's no lack,
but nothing with her is simple: there's always mess.
Diego feels like the parrot trained to say back
whatever she needs to hear, though meaningless.

Photograph not found online.

Frida Kahlo's Painting *Self-Portrait II*
 1940

Who cares about her thorn necklace?
Who cares if her neck bleeds from its thorns?
Diego screws women like he's doing porn.
Who cares about her thorn necklace?
When he screws them, he should see her face—
she wants him to wish he was never born.
Who cares about her thorn necklace?
Who cares if her neck bleeds from its thorns?

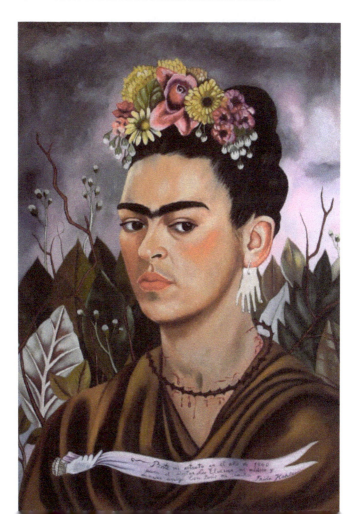

Frida Kahlo's Photo of Diego Rivera with Pet Spider Monkey

He feels Frida's the monkey, clinging to him.
He has to pry her hands loose from his neck.
When he's had enough, he becomes suspect.
He feels Frida's the monkey, clinging to him.
Diego's painted many women—rich, slim—
like Natasha Gelman, a lily in white dress.
He feels Frida's the monkey, clinging to him.
He has to pry her hands loose from his neck.

Photograph not found online.

Frida Kahlo's Lead Pencil Drawing of Her Bus Collision with the Trolley

Frida Kahlo, *The Accident, 17 September 1926*

The handrail went through her *like a sword through a bull*—
her description of how the metal took its course,
the boards splintering, tapping out DEATH in Morse—
the handrail went through her *like a sword through a bull*;
others were amputated (their death wasn't beautiful);
arm by leg by torso were assembled in due course.
The handrail went through her *like a sword through a bull*—
her description of how the metal took its course.

Frida Kahlo's Photo of Diego Rivera at La Casa Azul

> Frida Kahlo, *Diego Rivera in the Courtyard of La Casa Azul*, 1930

She said her other accident was meeting Diego:
that accident wounded heart as well as genitals—
his indifference was bad; the other women, hell.
She said her other accident was meeting Diego.
Time marches on—it takes you, and you go,
but where you end up, you can never tell.
She said her other accident was meeting Diego:
that accident wounded heart as well as genitals.

Héctor García's Photo of Frida Kahlo Asleep with Her Hairless Xoloitzcuintli Dog

Héctor García, *Frida Kahlo with Xoloitzcuintli Dog*, 1952

There is her partner, there is what she needs—
but sometimes El Señor Xolotl has had enough
(the way she won't let go, and all the other stuff).
There is her partner, there is what she needs.
Diego has a sandwich? El Señor Xolotl pleads—
she tightens her grip. (Even sleeping she is tough.)
There is her partner, there is what she needs—
but sometimes El Señor Xolotl has had enough.

For the photograph, search online with the title string, or go to https://www.artgallery.nsw.gov.au/artboards/frida-kahlo-diego-rivera/mexicanidad/item/4c7czn/.

Frida Kahlo's Painting *Remembrance of the Open Wound*

1938

She joked to a friend she was masturbating
which is why her right hand is hidden.
The unhealed wound in her thigh, men.
She joked to a friend she was masturbating.
But pleasure, she admitted, had to sting—
so what she regretted she would do again.
She joked to a friend she was masturbating
which is why her right hand is hidden.

Frida Kahlo's Painting *Self-Portrait in a Velvet Dress*

1926

Women are desired when they are young.
When they are young, they are all desire.
Between their legs there is always fire.
Women are desired when they are young.
With women, men want everything (for a song),
but having possessed them, they always tire.
Women are desired when they are young.
When they are young, they are all desire.

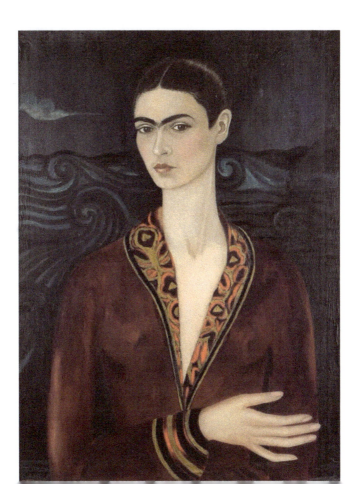

Frida Kahlo's Painting *Henry Ford Hospital* (Also Called *The Flying Bed*)

1932

It isn't that the body needs it to live.
Loss lives inside the body when life isn't.
Cacti bloom on schedule in the desert.
It isn't that the body needs it to live.
It was liquid; she, its cheesecloth sieve.
It does remain inside until it doesn't.
It isn't that the body needs it to live.
Loss lives inside the body when life isn't.

Frida Kahlo's Painting *Henry Ford Hospital* (Also Called *The Flying Bed*)

A uterus, a fetus, and a snail float
above where she knew she'd be
(what each stands for is no mystery).
A uterus, a fetus, and a snail float.
She counts dust in air, mote by mote—
time means nothing after you're empty.
A uterus, a fetus, and a snail float
above where she knew she'd be.

Frida Kahlo's Painting *Without Hope*

1945

The fetus was something she wanted back
but its mind made up, she was made unfit.
It gushed from her like so much vomit.
The fetus was something she wanted back.
She "could try again" to fill the empty sack,
a doctor told her, leaving the room unlit.
The fetus was something she wanted back
but its mind made up, she was made unfit.

Photo of Frida Kahlo with Butchered Hair and Wearing Male Attire

Guillermo Kahlo, *Frida Kahlo in Men's Clothing*, circa 1924

She won't discuss why her sister slept with him.
Diego knows who will or won't fall for his tricks.
Women can be cunts, but men are dicks.
She won't discuss why her sister slept with him.
She isn't being New Age or cosmopolitan—
she will be hard as males, only without a prick.
She won't discuss why her sister slept with him.
Diego knows who will or won't fall for his tricks.

Frida Kahlo's *Self-Portrait Very Ugly*
1933

What one loathes and desires can be the same thing.
Whom one loves and punishes can be one person.
Frida knows what women feel inside—undone.
What one loathes and desires can be the same thing.
Much too often, what she desires has to sting—
then her heart opens without it ever being open.
What one loathes and desires can be the same thing.
Whom one loves and punishes can be one person.

Frida Kahlo's Self-Portrait *Itzcuintli Dog with Me*

1938

This tiny dog was prized by the Aztecs.
They enslaved all, but not this little thing.
Bodies rolled down steps as offerings.
This tiny dog was prized by the Aztecs.
Diego tears out hearts—it's empowering
(obsidian is not the only way to open chests).
This tiny dog was prized by the Aztecs.
They enslaved all, but not this little thing.

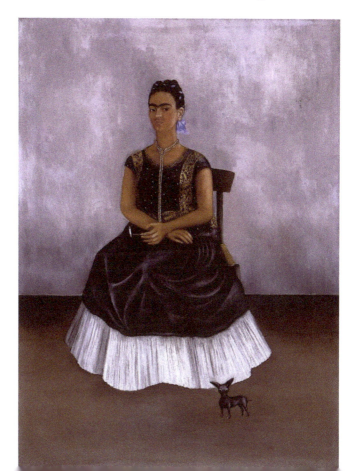

Frida Kahlo's Self-Portrait *Fulang-Chang and I*

1937

Fulang-Chang is one of her pet monkeys.
She has tied it to her with lavender ribbon.
Frida is a different Frida to every person—
not with Fulang-Chang, her pet monkey.
With him, her always being Frida is easy
(not with Diego, whose cock is a weapon).
Fulang-Chang is one of her pet monkeys.
She has tied it to her with lavender ribbon.

Tabloid Photo of Diego Rivera with Hollywood Actress Paulette Goddard

Photographer unknown, *Diego Rivera with Paulette Goddard*, 1940

It almost makes Frida want to turn her back.
Some gossip rag has caught him in some joint.
It almost makes her feel there is no point.
It almost makes Frida want to turn her back:
just another actress—him you want to smack;
she tells herself it's (not) her breakpoint.
It almost makes Frida want to turn her back.
Some gossip rag has caught him in some joint.

Frida Kahlo's Painting *Self-Portrait with Cropped Hair*

1940

She is the barber, barber-surgeon, and customer.
She has operated on herself for maximum damage.
Diego wants a divorce—he's turning the page.
She is the barber, barber-surgeon, and customer.
She's done as a woman—hair, all over the floor—
in male clothes, androgynous, of indeterminate age.
She is the barber, barber-surgeon, and customer.
She has operated on herself for maximum damage.

Frida Kahlo's Self-Portrait *Diego and I*
1949

She knows what he feels, she's part of him—
he's part her: he's her forehead's third eye.
She sees as he sees and doesn't have to try.
She knows what he feels, she's part of him.
She always smiles on black-and-white film
but life isn't black and white until you die.
She knows what he feels, she's part of him—
he's part her: he's her forehead's third eye.

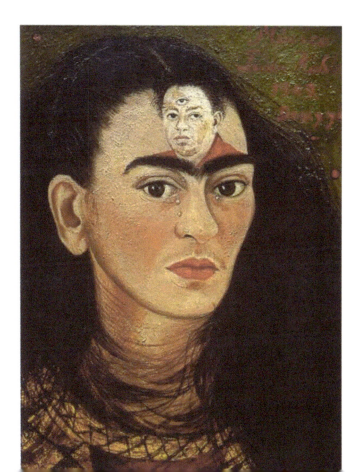

André Breton's Picnic Photo of Leon Trotsky, Trotsky's Wife Natalia Sedova, Diego Rivera, Frida Kahlo, and Himself

They pose as they wish to be seen by the camera:
they're all just friends trying to relax—
Ramón Mercader will smash in Trotsky's head with an ax.
Here, they pose as they wish to be seen by the camera.
That's the future—now, Trotsky and Frida have sex
(and he tells her the sex has never been better).
They pose as they wish to be seen by the camera.
They're all just friends trying to relax.

Photograph not found online.

Frida Kahlo's Painting *Between the Curtains* (Dedicated to Trotsky)

1937

Each woman is a suffragette.
Each sex act is a protest sign.
Each orgasm (real or not) designed.
Each woman is a suffragette.
Each woman remembers to forget.
Each partner in bed is a lifeline.
Each woman is a suffragette.
Each sex act is a protest sign.

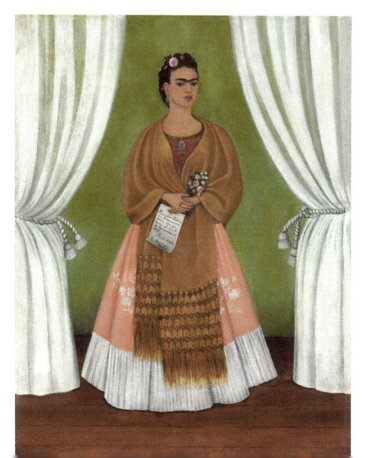

Nickolas Muray's Photo of Frida Kahlo with Her Pet Deer

Nickolas Muray, Frida with Granizo, Version 2, Coyoacan, 1939

She knows this is the pose everyone wants to see.
She puckers her lips to kiss her pet fawn Granizo.
She's sleeping with Nickolas; everyone sleeps with Diego.
She knows this is the pose everyone wants to see—
not with the cigarette; this time her hand is empty
(in an outtake, Granizo pulls away—she won't let go).
She knows this is the pose everyone wants to see.
She puckers her lips to kiss her pet fawn Granizo.

For the photograph, search online with the epigraph string, or go to https://nickolasmuray.com/archives/813/.

Nickolas Muray's Photo of Frida Kahlo with Chavela Vargas

1945

This is truly what gives women pleasure:
to rollick on a bed, convulsed with laughter,
clothes askew, each touching the other.
This is truly what gives women pleasure:
to have men look at them and not be sure
(is all this something innocent—or more?).
This is truly what gives women pleasure:
to rollick on a bed, convulsed with laughter.

    For the photograph, search online with the title string, or go to https://www.lazmagazine.com/single-post/2016/06/03/intimate-photographs-of-frida-kahlo (scroll down).

Colored Pencil Drawing of Frida Kahlo's Bus-Trolley Collision

It's possible to amputate the head through the neck
and to have the corpse look perfectly intact,
without injury—not one blemish—a fact.
It's possible to amputate the head through the neck.
The spinal column severs—outside, not a speck—
that is what a trolley collision can do on impact.
It's possible to amputate the head through the neck
and to have the corpse look perfectly intact.

Artwork is "Frida Kahlo's Colored Pencil Drawing of Her Bus Collision with a Trolley" on page 6.

Frida Kahlo's Teen Boyfriend's Memory of Her Bus-Trolley Collision

She was naked because it *tore off all of her clothes*;
a housepainter's bag of gold dust *burst over her body*.
People cried *la bailarina!*—the gold ballerina is bloody!
She was naked because it *tore off all of her clothes*.
People don't know when they'll die, no one knows—
a bloody gold ballerina can be the last thing you see.
She was naked because it *tore off all of her clothes*.
A housepainter's bag of gold dust *burst over her body*.

Frida Kahlo's Painting *The Suicide of Dorothy Hale*

1938

The best as worst appears to one at night:
the past as future, the future already past—
everything one desired didn't last;
the best as worst appears to one at night.
A B-list actress, a hanger-on socialite—
Hollywood to New York gossip at breakfast.
The best as worst appears to one at night:
the past as future, the future already past.

Frida Kahlo's Painting *The Suicide of Dorothy Hale*

She painted Dorothy's jump from the building tower—
not what Clare Boothe Luce commissioned
(a *recuerdo* is supposed to commemorate a friend).
She painted Dorothy's jump from the building tower.
This horrible painting no one could defend—
the leap, the fall, the sidewalk, the blood smear.
She painted Dorothy's jump from the building tower.
Not what Clare Boothe Luce commissioned.

Frida Kahlo's Nude Self-Portrait with Back Brace *The Broken Column*

1944

What makes you stronger will also kill you:
cracked ribs, shattered pelvis, a broken spine
(the machinery's nuts and bolts never on view).
What makes you stronger will also kill you.
But torture upright in bed is worse supine
when Diego stares and sees nothing to value.
What makes you stronger will also kill you:
cracked ribs, shattered pelvis, a broken spine.

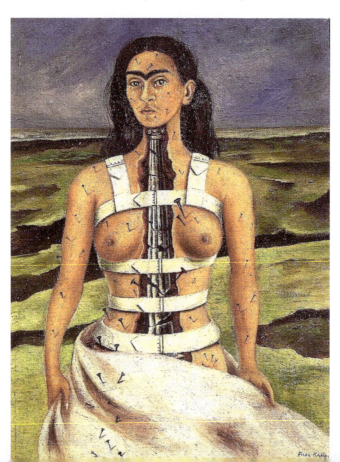

Photo of Frida Kahlo in Wheelchair Painting Her Self-Portrait *The Broken Column*

One day she'll stop jazzing all of them
with her brave suffering in that wheelchair
with Diego at her side stroking her hair.
One day she'll stop jazzing all of them—
and when she does, she'll finally tell him
what was never said: she did, and didn't, care.
One day she'll stop jazzing all of them
with her brave suffering in that wheelchair.

Photograph not found online.

Frida Kahlo's Self-Portraits with Her Parrots

Frida Kahlo, *Me and My Parrots*, 1941

Why does she need to treat them as human?
Her parrot's tongue in her mouth is not a kiss,
yet she wants each of them to remember this.
Why does she need to treat them as human?
She feels the same in bed with men and women—
she wants them to remember what they will miss.
Why does she need to treat them as human?
Her parrot's tongue in her mouth is not a kiss.

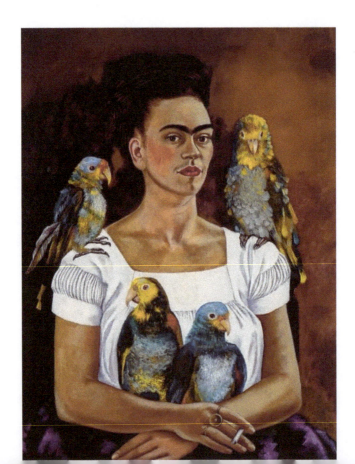

Frida Kahlo's Painting *Self-Portrait with Doll*
1937

She said this was the infant she did not get
but now it sat on the bed for all to see—
she too: white blouse, green skirt, with cigarette.
She said this was the infant she did not get.
In the miscarriage painting, there's no subtlety:
Frida spreads, head crowns, sheet goes bloody.
She said this was the infant she did not get
but now it sat on the bed for all to see.

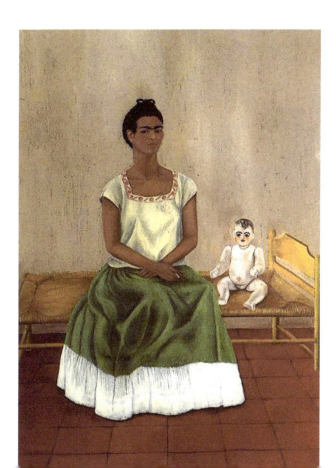

Frida Kahlo's Painting *A Few Small Nips* (*Passionately in Love*)

1935

The murderer, asked why he stabbed so many times,
responded that he had given her just *a few small nips*;
after she finds out what Diego did, Frida paints this
(to have had sex with her sister couldn't be dismissed).
She tells her friends, she felt like a witness to crime
(each time she saw them, her heart closed like a fist).
The murderer, asked why he stabbed so many times,
responded that he had given her just *a few small nips*.

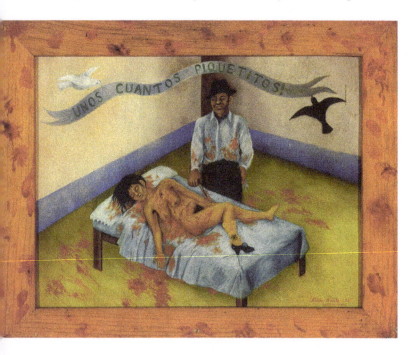

Frida Kahlo's Painting *Portrait of Diego Rivera*

1937

Who can say why one loves another?
Isn't what the heart desires complex?
With some it's talk; with others, sex.
Who can say why one loves another?
Diego's only human (he had a mother).
Why shouldn't one love one's ex?
Who can say why one loves another?
Isn't what the heart desires complex?

Photo of Frida Kahlo Flanked by Leon Trotsky and His Wife Natalia Sedova

Photographer unknown, 1937

She knows real revolution will not come
today, tomorrow, or in anyone's lifetime—
people are people; that is the real crime.
She knows real revolution will not come.
Meanwhile, his manifestos do help some
(and Leon tells her their sex is sublime).
She knows real revolution will not come
today, tomorrow, or in anyone's lifetime.

Deathbed Hospital Photo of Leon Trotsky

Photographer unknown, 1940

History is what the victors live to write.
Ramón smashed in Trotsky's skull with an ice pick.
Frida calls Diego in San Francisco—she's sick.
History is what the victors live to write.
She blames Diego—who's no longer a Trotskyite—
for driving Leon and Natalia from their home in panic.
History is what the victors live to write.
Ramón smashed in Trotsky's skull with an ice pick.

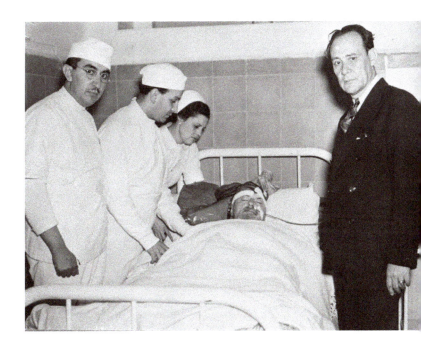

Photo of Frida Kahlo in Body Cast Painted with Soviet Hammer and Sickle

> Florence Arquin, *Frida Kahlo with Corset Painted with Fetus and Hammer & Sickle*, 1951

One day she's going to shake up everybody
and not just with her long skirts and rebozos,
those long shawls that everyone now knows.
One day she's going to shake up everybody—
she's going to make the motherfuckers see
all capitalists are just empty suits, just clothes.
One day she's going to shake up everybody
and not just with her long skirts and rebozos.

For the photograph, search online with the epigraph string, or go to https://throckmorton-nyc.com/project/florence-arquin/.

Frida Kahlo Photographed by Caricaturist Miguel Covarrubias

There's no caricature anywhere in this photo.
He's looking down at the suffering of a friend,
Frida in traction, lassoed at the top end.
There's no caricature anywhere in this photo.
What he sees will not be cover art for *Vogue*
(once more, she's stretched on the rack to mend).
There's no caricature anywhere in this photo.
He's looking down at the suffering of a friend.

Photograph not found online.

Photo of Diego Rivera and Frida Kahlo Reunited at La Casa Azul

Photographer unknown, 1940

Diego looks tired kissing her, lacking will.
He's been in bed, fearing kidney failure.
People want them to heal their rupture;
Diego looks tired kissing her, lacking will.
Once he defied Rockefeller with a mural
that included Lenin at Rockefeller Center
(long ago destroyed—money does what it will).
Diego looks tired, fearing kidney failure.

Photo of Frida Kahlo, Diego Rivera, and Pet Spider Monkey

One day he'll understand he didn't get it
and when that day comes it will be too late.
He holds her hand as if they're on a date.
One day he'll understand he didn't get it.
The monkey will break things if you let it.
Diego breaks everything and blames fate.
One day he'll understand he didn't get it
and when that day comes it will be too late.

Photograph not found online.

Photo of Frida Kahlo and Dr. Farill beside Her Painting *Self-Portrait with the Portrait of Dr. Farill*

Gisèle Freund, *Frida Kahlo and Dr. Juan Farill*, 1951

In her painting, her artist brushes drip blood.
She wants to heal, not die, and for pain to end.
In the painting, the palette is a heart sectioned.
In her painting, her artist brushes drip blood.
In the photo, on a wheelchair wheel is dried mud
(she doesn't know the last surgery has happened).
In her painting, her artist brushes drip blood.
She wants to heal, not die, and for pain to end.

    For the photograph, search online with the epigraph string, or go to https://chicago.suntimes.com/2022/3/30/23001838/frida-kahlo-photo-exhibit-photography-national-museum-of-mexican-art-chicago/.

Wallace Marly's Photo of Frida Kahlo and Diego Rivera Reunited

1944

Again, there is the pet monkey joining them:
it clings to Diego, Frida scratches its fur—
a family once more, that's what it means to her.
Again, there is the pet monkey joining them.
Frida knows Diego's sex life, and outdoes him:
she fucked several of his mistresses, and others.
Again, there is the pet monkey joining them—
it clings to Diego, Frida scratches its fur.

    For the photograph, search online with the title string, or go to https://www.pinterest.cl/pin/290763719672679779/.

Late Photo of Frida Kahlo Propped Up in Bed Painting as Diego Rivera Looks On

Photographer unknown, 1952

She knows nothing can undo the damage.
She smiles, the paintbrush smiles, Diego smiles
(in her painting, everything smiles); all the while,
she also knows nothing can undo the damage.
The dead are not at peace—they're full of rage
(pretending she was someone else was infantile).
She knows nothing can undo the damage.
She smiles, the paintbrush smiles, Diego smiles.

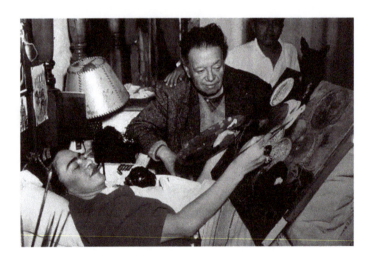

Late Frida Kahlo's Colored Pencil Drawing of the Bus-Trolley Accident

Someday the handrail won't go through her pelvis.
Some other day she will get on that bus
and go someplace, but not because she must.
Someday the handrail won't go through her pelvis—
or if the trolley strikes, the handrail will miss
and she will have children and be a great artist.
Someday the handrail won't go through her pelvis.
Some other day she will get on that bus.

Artwork is "Frida Kahlo's Colored Pencil Drawing of Her Bus Collision with a Trolley" on page 6.

Frida Kahlo's Self-Portraits with Her Parrots

Frida Kahlo, *Self-Portrait with Bonito*, 1941

What does it mean when the parrot you love feeds you?
What does it mean when it unselfishly gives back?
Too often, people envy in others what they lack.
What does it mean when the parrot you love feeds you?
She envied everyone, but tried to keep that from view
(at least she tried, but it was hard to keep track).
What does it mean when the parrot you love feeds you?
What does it mean when it unselfishly gives back?

Late Photo of Frida Kahlo in Her Wheelchair

Photographer unknown, 1952

Someday she'll be able to throw out the narcotics
with her back brace and all its straps and wiring
and say *fuck it* to all the ugliness and everything.
Someday she'll be able to throw out the narcotics—
flush it all down the toilet with all the bullshit
and keep on flushing until there's no more ring.
Someday she'll be able to throw out the narcotics
with her back brace and all its straps and wiring.

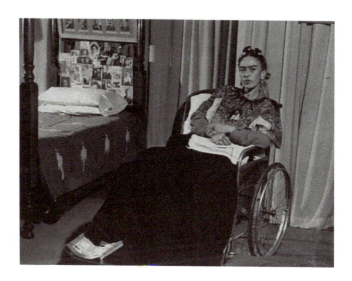

Julien Levy's Photo of Frida Kahlo Looking Off into the Distance

He's used to it, her dining with the dead.
For her, there's no time like *now* or *was*
(past is present for what she feels or does).
He's used to it, her dining with the dead.
She brings sugar skulls, empanadas, bread,
spoons their beans, holds their beverages.
He's used to it, her dining with the dead.
For her, there's no time like *now* or *was*.

Photograph not found online.

Photo of Diego Rivera at Frida Kahlo's Deathbed

He said it was his most disgusting trait—
the more she loved, the more he wanted to hurt.
With women, he always had to find the dirt.
He said it was his most disgusting trait—
To love them intensely and then to hate,
to have to know what was beneath every skirt.
He said it was his most disgusting trait—
the more she loved, the more he wanted to hurt.

Photograph not found online.

Photo of Young Frida Kahlo beside Diego Rivera Seated in Chair with Stetson on His Knee

Nickolas Muray, *Frida and Diego with Hat*, 1941

Who can explain whom and why you love?
Who can explain the moment it happens?
Who can explain why it's men or women?
Who can explain whom and why you love?
The marriage of an elephant to a dove—
that's what her mother said seeing this man.
Who can explain whom and why you love?
Who can explain the moment it happens?

For the photograph, search online with the title string, or go to https://collections.telfair.org/objects/6798/frida-and-diego-with-hat/.

Frida Kahlo's Painting *Girl with Death Mask (She Plays Alone)*

1938

The broken child will one day be adult.
She will please no one, and everyone she can.
She will climb into bed with a man or woman.
The broken child will one day be adult.
During her lifetime you see her molt,
each relationship like an exoskeleton.
The broken child will one day be adult.
She will please no one, and everyone she can.

Self-Portrait Photo of Frida Kahlo at Her Reflection Pool

She thought it could never happen, but it did.
No one was there to see it except her.
She wished that others could have seen the water.
She thought it could never happen, but it did,
herself reflected there—but then it hid:
as if her reflection were someone other.
She thought it could never happen, but it did.
No one was there to see it except her.

Photograph not found online.

Frida Kahlo's Painting *Tree of Hope*

1946

The dream of the two Fridas is everyone's dream:
at left, the surgical back; at right, the brace not needed—
no regrets (for omissions, not only for what one did);
the dream of the two Fridas is everyone's dream.
At left, on the gurney she suppresses a scream.
At right, finally whole, she faces us, completed.
The dream of the two Fridas is everyone's dream:
at left, the surgical back; at right, the brace not needed.

Gisèle Freund's Photo of Frida Kahlo at La Casa Azul

This is the photo to capture her success.
This is the publicity shoot for everyone.
Frida is feeding the ducks in her garden.
This is the photo to capture her success,
but look behind, at the Maya statuettes:
warriors who cut to bone with obsidian.
This is the photo to capture her success.
This is the publicity shoot for everyone.

For the photograph, search online with the title string, or go to https://news.artnet.com/market/frida-kahlo-photos-by-edward-weston-at-throckmorton-278571/#/slideshow/278571-0/6/.

Photo of Frida Kahlo's Casket Being Carried from the Palace of Fine Arts

Photographer unknown, 1954

She said that she had forgotten why she ever married
but you can endure much more than you think you can:
she said her life was always healed or broken by one man.
She said that she had forgotten why she ever married.
She said that she never expected to live after she died.
She said she had embraced chaos—there had been no plan.
She said that she had forgotten why she ever married
but you can endure much more than you think you can.

Stephen Gibson's seventh collection, *Self-Portrait in a Door-Length Mirror* (University of Arkansas Press, 2017), won the Miller Williams Poetry Prize, selected by Billy Collins. Earlier collections include *The Garden of Earthly Delights: Book of Ghazals* (Texas Review Press, 2016); *Rorschach Art Too* (Story Line Press, 2014; reprint, Red Hen Press Legacy Title, 2021), winner of the Donald Justice Prize; *Paradise* (University of Arkansas Press, 2011), finalist for the Miller Williams Poetry Prize; *Frescoes* (Lost Horse Press, 2011), winner of the Idaho Prize for Poetry; *Masaccio's Expulsion* (Intuit House, 2008), winner of the MARGIE Book Prize; and *Rorschach Art* (Red Hen Press, 2001). His poems have appeared in such journals as *Able Muse, American Arts Quarterly*, the *American Journal of Poetry, Boulevard, Cimarron Review, Copper Nickel, Court Green*, the *Evansville Review, EPOCH, Field*, the *Gettysburg Review*, the *Hudson Review*, the *Iowa Review, J Journal, Measure, New England Review, Notre Dame Review*, the *Paris Review, Pleiades, Ploughshares, Poetry, Prairie Schooner, Quiddity, Raleigh Review, Salamander*, the *Sewanee Review, Shenandoah, Southern Poetry Review*, the *Southern Review*, the *Southwest Review, Upstreet*, the *Yale Review*, and elsewhere.

Also from Able Muse Press

Jacob M. Appel, *The Cynic in Extremis: Poems*

William Baer, *Times Square and Other Stories; New Jersey Noir: A Novel;*
   New Jersey Noir (Cape May): A Novel;
   New Jersey Noir (Barnegat Light): A Novel
   New Jersey Noir (Shippen Manor): A Novel

Lee Harlin Bahan, *A Year of Mourning: Sonnets (Petrarch): Translation;*
   Advent and Lent: Sestinas and Sonnets (Petrarch): Translation

Melissa Balmain, *Walking in on People (Able Muse Book Award for Poetry)*

Ben Berman, *Strange Borderlands: Poems; Figuring in the Figure: Poems;*
   Writing While Parenting: Essays

David Berman, *Progressions of the Mind: Poems*

Lorna Knowles Blake, *Green Hill (Able Muse Book Award for Poetry)*

Michael Cantor, *Life in the Second Circle: Poems*

Catherine Chandler, *Lines of Flight: Poems*

William Conelly, *Uncontested Grounds: Poems*

Maryann Corbett, *Credo for the Checkout Line in Winter: Poems;*
   Street View: Poems; In Code: Poems

Will Cordeiro, *Trap Street (Able Muse Book Award for Poetry)*

Brian Culhane, *Remembering Lethe: Poems*

John Philip Drury, *Sea Level Rising: Poems; The Teller's Cage: Poems*

Josh Dugat, *Great and Small: Poems*

Gregory Emilio, *Kitchen Apocrypha: Poems*

Rhina P. Espaillat, *And After All: Poems*

Anna M. Evans, *Under Dark Waters: Surviving the* Titanic: *Poems*

Nicole Caruso Garcia, *Oxblood: Poems*

Amy Glynn, *Romance Language (Able Muse Book Award for Poetry)*

D. R. Goodman, *Greed: A Confession: Poems*

Carrie Green, *Studies of Familiar Birds: Poems*

Margaret Ann Griffiths, *Grasshopper: The Poetry of M A Griffiths*

Janis Harrington, *How to Cut a Woman in Half: Poems*

Katie Hartsock, *Bed of Impatiens: Poems; Wolf Trees: Poems*

Elise Hempel, *Second Rain: Poems*

Jan D. Hodge, *Taking Shape: Carmina figurata;*
   The Bard & Scheherazade Keep Company: Poems; Finesse: Verse and Anagram

Stephen Kampa, *World Too Loud to Hear: Poems*

Ellen Kaufman, *House Music: Poems; Double-Parked, with Tosca: Poems*

Len Krisak, *Say What You Will (Able Muse Book Award for Poetry)*

Emily Leithauser, *The Borrowed World (Able Muse Book Award for Poetry)*

Hailey Leithauser, *Saint Worm: Poems*

Carol Light, *Heaven from Steam: Poems*

Kate Light, *Character Shoes: Poems*

April Lindner, *This Bed Our Bodies Shaped: Poems*

David Livewell, *Pass and Stow: Poems*
Susan McLean, *Daylight Losing Time: Poems*
Martin McGovern, *Bad Fame: Poems*
Jeredith Merrin, *Cup: Poems*
Richard Moore, *Selected Poems;*
  The Rule That Liberates: An Expanded Edition: Selected Essays
Richard Newman, *All the Wasted Beauty of the World: Poems*
Alfred Nicol, *Animal Psalms: Poems*
Deirdre O'Connor, *The Cupped Field (Able Muse Book Award for Poetry)*
Frank Osen, *Virtue, Big as Sin (Able Muse Book Award for Poetry)*
Alexander Pepple (Editor), *Able Muse Anthology;*
  Able Muse: A Review of Poetry, Prose & Art (semiannual, winter 2010 on)
James Pollock, *Sailing to Babylon: Poems*
Aaron Poochigian, *The Cosmic Purr: Poems; Manhattanite*
  (Able Muse Book Award for Poetry)
Tatiana Forero Puerta, *Cleaning the Ghost Room: Poems*
Jennifer Reeser, *Indigenous: Poems; Strong Feather: Poems*
John Ridland, *Sir Gawain and the Green Knight (Anonymous): Translation;*
  Pearl (Anonymous): Translation
Kelly Rowe, *Rise above the River (Able Muse Book Award for Poetry)*
Stephen Scaer, *Pumpkin Chucking: Poems*
Hollis Seamon, *Corporeality: Stories*
Ed Shacklee, *The Blind Loon: A Bestiary*
Carrie Shipers, *Cause for Concern (Able Muse Book Award for Poetry)*
Gabriel Spera, *Twisted Pairs: Poems*
Matthew Buckley Smith, *Dirge for an Imaginary World*
  (Able Muse Book Award for Poetry)
Susan de Sola, *Frozen Charlotte: Poems*
Barbara Ellen Sorensen, *Compositions of the Dead Playing Flutes: Poems*
Rebecca Starks, *Time Is Always Now: Poems; Fetch, Muse: Poems*
Sally Thomas, *Motherland: Poems*
Paulette Demers Turco (Editor), *The Powow River Poets Anthology II*
Rosemerry Wahtola Trommer, *Naked for Tea: Poems*
Wendy Videlock, *Nevertheless: Poems; The Dark Gnu and Other Poems;*
  Slingshots and Love Plums: Poems; Wise to the West: Poems
Richard Wakefield, *A Vertical Mile: Poems; Terminal Park: Poems*
Gail White, *Asperity Street: Poems*
Chelsea Woodard, *Vellum: Poems*
Rob Wright, *Last Wishes: Poems*

www.ablemusepress.com

www.ingramcontent.com/pod-product-compliance
Lightning Source LLC
Chambersburg PA
CBHW041143200325
23810CB00021B/1630